South East Bus Memories in Colour
By Bob Jackson

Copyright IRWELL PRESS Ltd.,
ISBN 978-1-906919-14-6
First published in 2010 by Irwell Press Ltd., 59A, High Street, Clophill, Bedfordshire, MK45 4BE
Printed by Konway Press

I think I first developed an interest in buses at the age of five whilst staying with my grandparents in Yardley, Birmingham. They never owned a car, so all journeys were either on foot or by Corporation bus and I was soon able to differentiate between exposed or concealed radiator, although I was unaware at the time which make of chassis lay behind it. With my father serving in the Royal Navy, periods were spent in Preston (Ribble), Gosport (Provincial) and Helensburgh (Garelochhead) with daily journeys to school on the mainly second-hand buses of the last named operator. We eventually returned to Portsmouth, the trolleybuses having been retired seven years previously, and after completing my formal education I approached Southdown Motor Services Ltd to see if they 'had any jobs'. I received an encouraging letter back saying the company had granted me an interview with the Traffic Manager, who would travel down from Brighton to meet me at the offices in Winston Churchill Avenue, still shown on my map as Hyde Park Road. I was duly enrolled into the company's Junior Management Training Scheme and took up the duties of Booking Clerk, at a wage of £10 per week, selling coach tickets for travel to all parts of Britain. This was in the days before National Express, and services in the Coach Guide were grouped by operator rather than destination so I soon got to know the geographical location of many of the bus companies I had seen listed in the 'Fleet News' section of my favourite monthly magazine. As my career progressed, I also spent informative periods at Central Works and Head Office, followed by postings to depots in East and West Sussex.

Seeking a new challenge, I then joined a small coach firm in Hampshire before the usual trappings of life demanded that I earn a regular income which, in the event, came to be provided by the City of Portsmouth Passenger Transport Department. As many people will know, this was the first council owned bus company to be sold to the private sector and after a period working for the new regime, famous for its 'bread vans', I had decided that there was nothing quite like being around 'proper' buses. The nearest operator of these was a relative newcomer from Scotland, which very kindly gave me an opportunity I have never regretted taking.

I was persuaded to write this book by my very good friend Paul Roberts, whose name you will have seen on other titles in this series. It is not intended to be a photographic record of every bus operator in the South East, more a selection of views that I took during my travels in the early to mid-1970s. All are from colour transparencies, or slides, as these were relatively cheap to have processed compared with colour prints. It may have been inconvenient to set up the projector to show them to friends but compensation came in the form of the lively discussions which generally ensued. I do not take many photographs nowadays, as the quality of digital images available in print or on-line is so good as to put my humble efforts to shame. I also have to admit to having lost track, to a certain extent, of who owns what and I am not a fan of some of the rather less inspired liveries to be seen in some parts of the country. The photographs that follow are arranged so as to take the reader on a clockwise circular tour of Hampshire, Surrey, Kent and Sussex although I have deliberately avoided straying into London Transport territory, which has been more than well covered by many other, more knowledgeable, authors. Thanks are due to Paul Roberts for the numerous telephone calls and e-mails of encouragement, and to my wife, Linda, for deciphering my hand written scribbles.

Bob Jackson
Portsmouth 2010

Hiding away in East Kent's Westwood depot, midway between Margate and Ramsgate, is AEC Regent V PFN 882. Numerically the last of a batch of 40 delivered in 1959, the Park Royal body has 72 seats accessed by a large air-operated sliding door behind the front wheel. The 'pay as you enter' sign on the radiator grill indicates that this vehicle could be one-man operated.

Stepping off the ferry from Portsmouth, the traveller emerges into Gosport bus station where, during the latter part of the 1970s, the standard fare in the 'Provincial' fleet was the ubiquitous Leyland National produced at a new factory in Workington. Following acquisition by the National Bus Company, inroads were quickly made into the mixed fleet of Guy rebuilds that had long been the trademark of the Gosport and Fareham Omnibus Company. The first new standard vehicles to appear were twelve dual-door Bristol REs in 1971-72, after which batches of dual-door 44-seat Nationals arrived each year up until 1980. By 1981, following withdrawal of the REs, apart from two second-hand Bristol LHs the fleet consisted entirely of products from the Workington plant. This particular bus, fleet number 23 (PCG 923M) was written-off in an accident and its place taken in 1988 by a similar, ex-Southdown, vehicle RUF 37R which was, for a number of years, owned by the author.

During the late 1960s it became apparent that the ten re-bodied AEC Regals, some of them with chassis dating from 1934, were reaching the end of their useful lives. In 1968, following a change of policy, an order was placed for nine Seddon Pennine IV chassis to be fitted with Southampton-built Strachans 40-seater bodies. Whilst not ideal for town service work, with noisy front-mounted Perkins engines, manual gearboxes and high steps, they at least brought a degree of modernity to the Provincial fleet. The following year a further six were delivered, this time with Seddon's own Pennine Coachcraft bodywork, which were much less attractive and proved less durable than the Strachans examples, being withdrawn when less than seven years old. Several of the earlier batch gained NBC livery including 46 (MHO 195F), laying-over at the Ferry bus station, which finally bowed out in 1977.

In April 1973 the business of R. Chisnell and Sons, trading as King Alfred Motor Services, was acquired by the National Bus Company and its fleet was merged with that of Hants and Dorset operating from Winchester Depot. Several vehicles were taken into stock including three Metro-Scania single-deckers; being non-standard in the south of England they were exchanged for Leyland Nationals from the London Country fleet which already operated this type in the Stevenage area. The three immigrants were easily recognizable by their green livery and were the only Hants and Dorset Nationals to have separate entrance and exit doors. 1972-built 3627 (NPD 111L) was previously London Country LN11 and is seen on a wet day in Fareham bus station waiting to return to its new home city, no doubt accompanied by the stern-looking lady with the shopping bag. On the left of the picture, an early Southdown Bristol VRT on route 347 loads for Southsea, whilst a Vauxhall Victor FB estate car almost escapes from the viewfinder.

For a number of years, Southampton was well known for its large fleet of Guy Arabs and, robust as they were, replacements were eventually forthcoming in the shape of Leyland PD2s and AEC Regent Vs. In the event, the Regent was the preferred choice and 70 were delivered between 1963 and 1967, initially with Park Royal or East Lancs bodies seating 66, but thereafter on longer chassis accommodating a further ten passengers. In this view one of the 76-seaters, 368 (BOW 504C), rounds the corner from New Road into Above Bar Street whilst running empty from Portswood depot to the city centre to take up service on the 15 to Bassett Green and Swaythling. The conductor, who is preparing himself for the onslaught, hangs on tightly, the Neepsend body heeling over as the driver avoids the 'keep left' bollard.

Southampton Corporation had two garages; the smaller, an ex-tram depot, was in Carlisle Road, Shirley, although it was sometimes referred to as Newman Street. It housed mainly crew buses, with the majority being stored in the open as evident in this Sunday morning shot of 331 (331 AOW), a 1963 Leyland Titan PD2A/27, with rather square Park Royal 66-seat body. A small letter 's', denoting the Shirley depot allocation, is just visible on the cream band above the front canopy. Thirty-two Titans were purchased between 1961 and 1963, with the earlier examples sporting the less fussy Midland Red style bonnet. They had all gone before the last conductor-operated routes were converted to one-man operation in 1981, and Shirley depot is now but a memory.

From 1968, the appearance of the first of a large fleet of Leyland Atlanteans, along with a few AEC and Seddon single-deckers, saw the introduction of a new, brighter livery with more cream and a lighter shade of red. Crew buses, however, continued to be painted in their traditional colours. Approaching the city centre on route 2A from Lords Hill is 1969-built Atlantean PDR1A/1 no.135 (TTR 169H) with an East Lancashire Coachbuilders 76-seat body. Southampton eventually amassed 175 of this type bought new, plus a few second-hand examples with different bodywork from Portsmouth and Plymouth. They lasted until 2005 with their final days of operation being much reported in the enthusiast press. The ABC cinema in the background obviously catered for diverse tastes offering a choice of *The Outlaw Josey Wales* or, on screen 2, *Erotic Inferno*!

Upon the formation of the National Bus Company in 1969, both Hants & Dorset Motor Services Ltd and Wilts & Dorset came under common management with new vehicles thereafter registered in Bournemouth. Wilts & Dorset buses were Tilling red, as opposed to the green of the larger fleet, and were allocated fleet numbers in a separate series below 1000, although batches of similar buses were shared between the two companies. In 1972, the Wilts & Dorset name was dropped and all subsequent repaints were into NBC poppy red. Still in original livery, but now with cream Hants & Dorset fleet names, is 534 (XEL 838K), one of 127 ECW bodied Bristol LHs delivered new to both fleets over a period of seven years. In addition, 42 similar vehicles were later acquired from Bristol Omnibus Company. This 1972 example, outstationed at Romsey, has 43 seats although some earlier, flat-windscreen vehicles had only 39 seats and two doorways. Fairly primitive in design, with a manual gearbox and a rather bouncy ride, the LH was, none the less, reliable and simple to maintain with many surplus vehicles later finding their way to independent operators. The Ford Transit minibus behind originated with the King Alfred business.

Emerging from beneath the rather grandiose sign, which spans the exit from Winchester bus station, is Bristol Lodekka LD6G no.1482 operating a local route previously the responsibility of King Alfred Motor Services. By 1976, when this picture was taken, the bus had lost its upper deck cream band and black mudguards in favour of a scheme which was presumably quicker to apply when repainting was due. In early 1960, part way through the YRU registration series, Lodekka deliveries changed to the new FS type which had a step-free lower saloon floor, a feature no doubt appreciated by many residents of Bournemouth, where Hants & Dorset's head office was situated. Just to the left of the 58-seat ECW body can be seen what might correctly be termed a 'mobility vehicle', once a common sight on Britain's roads but nowadays virtually extinct.

Red alternates with green in this view of the parking area at the rear of Hants & Dorset's Winchester bus station, where one could hazard a fairly accurate guess as to which colour identifies the lucky hopefuls who will remain in the fleet for a few more years. As well as a Leyland National, a Bristol MW and several Lodekkas, the front-entrance versions of which have the more upright front profile, a pair of ex-King Alfred vehicles are also in evidence. SCG 855 is a 1957 Leyland Tiger Cub with a Weymann body featuring 41 dual purpose (semi-coach type) seats whilst WCG 106 alongside is an AEC Bridgemaster of the early rear-entrance design dating from 1959. The 74-seat body is by Park Royal and was unusual at the time as it formed the structural support for the various mechanical units, the vehicle having no separate chassis. The Bridgemaster was intended to be a provincial version of London's Routemaster but, in the event, sales were disappointing with most operators continuing to place body and chassis orders with different manufacturers.

As well as the Bridgemasters, King Alfred took delivery of two of its successor model, the AEC Renown which, though still bodied by Park Royal, had reverted to the traditional construction method of separate chassis and body. This vehicle, reversing off the stand in Winchester, remained in service with Hants & Dorset until 1976 and is now preserved, along with its sister 595 LCG, as part of the 'Friends of King Alfred Buses' collection. The poppy red paint used by National Bus Company subsidiaries was a particularly bright shade when freshly applied, but had a tendency to fade after a couple of years, especially in the case of factory spray finishes. The 'Wanderbus' ticket, nowadays called an 'Explorer', had actually gone up to £1.50 by the time this photograph was taken. The price had therefore more than doubled since its introduction in 1974.

Puzzled locals may have looked long and hard in an attempt to find the Alder Valley on their Ordnance Survey maps, as the name was merely an amalgam of the two NBC-owned companies brought together under one management in January 1972. In fact, a more appropriate geographical name might have been 'Blackwater Valley', as this lies between Aldershot & District's base in Aldershot and Thames Valley's headquarters in Reading. In between duties at the former location is 1971 Bristol RELL6G no.444 carrying a 44-seat dual-door body built by Marshall of Cambridge. Although arguably more attractive than the standard Eastern Coach Works bodies usually associated with the RE chassis, the Marshall product suffered from corrosion around the front and rear overhangs and was therefore not generally as long-lived. Behind, one of only twelve ECW bodied RESLs delivered to Aldershot & District the same year, awaits mechanical attention, perhaps from one of the fitters the company was hoping to recruit by means of the advertisement poster on the side of 444!

Resting at the back of Aldershot depot, on an area now occupied by housing, is 1954 AEC Reliance MU3RV MOR586 carrying the new company fleet name over the old Aldershot & District colours. The bus was originally numbered 255, fitted with a Strachans 41-seat centre-entrance coach body, but was one of fifteen similar vehicles reclothed by Metro-Cammell in 1967 to alleviate a shortage of single-deckers suitable for one-man operation. When re-delivered in its new guise it arrived just in time to wear the company's standard bus livery with dark green roof and light green lower panels but, by the time the camera catches it shortly after withdrawal, it has gained the final version with the dark and light green areas reversed. Aldershot & District continued to purchase Reliances for bus work until 1969, with bodywork by Weymann, Park Royal, Metro-Cammell, Willowbrook and Marshall, until vehicle policy changed in favour of the rear-engined Bristol RE model.

One of the final batch of 50 Dennis Loline IIIs delivered in 1964, Thames Valley and Aldershot Omnibus Company no.826 (499KOT) was originally 499 in the Aldershot & District fleet. The 68-seat Weymann body is arguably more attractively proportioned than the Alexander product specified for previous batches and the drab maroon livery, introduced in January 1972 but replaced by National Bus Company poppy red only a year later, appears less uninspiring than it did when applied to other vehicles owned by the company. On a cold January day in 1976, a small group of passengers waits in the shelter at Guildford's rather depressing Onslow Street bus station for the crew to return from their break, start the Gardner 6LW engine and plod off in the direction of Wood Street, a small hamlet two and a half miles west of the town centre. One-man operation soon ousted the last of the conductors and the arrival of more Bristol VRs ensured that all remaining Lolines had been withdrawn by the end of 1980, having survived well beyond their planned 12-year life-span.

Horsham has been served by a multitude of operators over the years, and was the point where passengers taking advantage of the travel opportunities afforded by the new 'Wanderbus' ticket could transfer from their Southdown bus on to a London Country or Alder Valley vehicle, depending on their chosen destination. Services met in the historic area known as 'the Carfax' and, in this February 1976 view, the smart poppy red livery on recently delivered Leyland National no.218 helps to brighten up the otherwise colourless scene. The reflections on the side windows are from the neon signs of the café opposite. Alder Valley was in desperate need of new buses, and the large influx of Nationals helped displace the aging AEC Reliances and Bristol MWs inherited with the Aldershot & District and Thames Valley fleets. This particular bus passed, with the later privatised business, to Stagecoach in 1992, becoming 1218 in its Hants & Surrey fleet. Upon withdrawal it was purchased for preservation and can now be seen regularly on the rally circuit.

In contrast to the previous view, but taken on the same day, is London Country Bus Services AEC Swift 3P2R, stock number MB110, wearing the leaf green version of the NBC's standard bus livery. A rather curious colour, leaf green appeared to come in several shades dependant upon paint manufacturer, and whether the finish had been sprayed or brush applied. The MB class of vehicles was inherited from London Transport in 1970 and the first examples, dubbed 'Merlin' by the London Passenger Transport Board (presumably as they would work wonders for London's public transport system), arrived in 1966 in a blaze of publicity. By 1973, however, withdrawals had commenced as LT had decided they were too expensive to recertify for further service, and Swift deliveries had already been switched to the shorter, more manoeuvrable SM type. London Country's MBs fared better as, at this time, the company had an acute shortage of vehicles suitable for one-man operation and MB110, pictured on a Horsham local service, lasted until 1979. The 45-seat dual-door Metro-Cammell Weymann body displays a Reigate garage allocation code above the front wheel arch.

Like many municipal operators, Maidstone Corporation's earliest venture into public transport came when it began its first tram services, in 1904. By 1930 the three tram routes had been replaced by a small trolleybus system, four vehicles from which are now preserved, and this was augmented, to a lesser extent, by a few motorbuses. In 1956, Leyland PD2 no.1 arrived, beginning a new fleet number series, and further small batches of Massey bodied PD2s were delivered each year until 1963, when the final four PD2As sporting St Helens-style bonnets were placed in service. The last of this batch, no.26, was captured in Maidstone High Street on a late Saturday afternoon wearing the pale blue livery which was introduced with the arrival of the Atlanteans, thereby replacing the previous tan and cream. The rear-entrance body had room for 61 seated passengers within its 27-foot length, and was not equipped with a route number blind, the system being small enough to manage without.

In 1965 Maidstone commenced its trolleybus replacement programme following the arrival of the first batch of Leyland Atlanteans numbered 27 to 34. As with the PD2s, the chosen coachbuilder was Massey Brothers of Wigan who produced this rather unimaginative but functional design. Eventually acquiring twenty similar vehicles, Maidstone was the main recipient of this combination with only Colchester and A1 of Ardrossan specifying a similar product. More would doubtless have followed but, in 1967, Massey Brothers was taken over by Northern Counties, its rather larger manufacturing neighbour, and the final eight Atlanteans therefore came fitted with NCME bodywork. The bigger surprise was in 1974 when the undertaking (the old-fashioned name for a council-owned bus company), by now trading as Maidstone Borough Council, announced that all future orders would be for lightweight single-deckers, Bedford being the chosen supplier. By 1978 the Atlanteans, some no more than six years old, had all gone. In this view, no.34 (EKP 234C) shows off the angular lines of its 75-seat body having been pressed into service before its replacement panels had even seen the painter's brush.

Caught in traffic in Maidstone High Street is Maidstone & District 6080, formerly DL80 prior to the 1968 fleet renumbering. The letter 'L' denotes low overall height. M&D was an early user of rear-engined vehicles, having amassed a fleet of 192 Leyland Atlanteans and Daimler Fleetlines by the time one-man operation of double-deckers became legal in 1966. Representing the latter type, 6080 has a Gardner 6LX engine and 77-seat Northern Counties body, being one of a batch of 35 delivered in 1963 hard on the heels of batches of Atlanteans of both low and normal height. The Daimler scored over its Lancashire-built rival in having a drop-centre rear axle which permitted a stepless lower saloon gangway and thus a conventional seating layout upstairs, as opposed to the semi-lowbridge arrangement necessary on early low-height Atlanteans. Despite the 'pay as you enter' sign, the bus appears to have a conductor who engages the driver in conversation as he sits back to keep the sun from his eyes. Two Hillman cars from different eras follow behind, no doubt hardly visible to the bus driver in the rather quaint round mirrors fitted to his vehicle.

Following the formation of the National Bus Company in 1969, of which both East Kent Road Car Company and Maidstone & District Motor Services became subsidiaries, a joint manufacturing company was created by Leyland and NBC with the aim of mass-producing a standard single-decker bus which would appeal to passengers, drivers and bus company engineers alike. The result was the Leyland National, an integral vehicle of riveted steel construction, assembled at a brand new factory in Workington, Cumbria. Following prototype trials, production models began arriving at their often less than enthusiastic operators from late 1972, initially all to the standard length of 11.3 metres but with a choice of one or two doorways. This, of course, would have been 37ft 1in, but the components were all metric, a complete departure from previous British design; Leyland hoped this would generate export orders as well as sales for the home market. The green vehicle, photographed at Maidstone Bus station in 1974, is 3502, numerically the second delivery to Maidstone & District. It would eventually form part of a fleet of 70 such vehicles, including one acquired from Southdown in 1974. The East Kent bus, a slightly newer example, carries no fleet number as these were not introduced until five years later when it became 1070. East Kent eventually acquired 119 Leyland Nationals, 35 of which were to the shorter length of 10.3m.

East Kent was not an early convert to rear-engined double-deckers, persisting with the tried and trusted AEC Regent V until 1967, when the reality dawned of their unsuitability for wholesale conversion to one-man operation. A year and a half later, twenty Daimler Fleetlines duly arrived carrying 72-seat bodywork by Park Royal Vehicles, the favoured supplier, and these entered service on Thanet area routes. A further fifteen Fleetlines were ordered for delivery in 1971 but in the event these were diverted to Southdown, receiving Eastern Coach Works bodies and the numbers 385-399 in that fleet. East Kent purchased no further double-deckers until 1976 when fifteen Leyland Atlantean AN68s appeared, although four early PDR1 models had been acquired from Maidstone & District in 1974 in exchange for Regent Vs. In this March 1976 view, 959 is inside the company's Westwood garage still wearing the traditional dark red and cream fleet livery. Its sister behind has succumbed to a coat of the new NBC poppy red.

Also still displaying the traditional company livery is 1965-built AEC Reliance 2U3RA, DJG610C, with a 49-seat Park Royal body adapted for one-man operation. The Reliance had been a firm favourite with East Kent since 1955 and featured in the company's vehicle buying policy for twenty years, by which time 375 had been delivered. Early examples were 30 feet in length and were 'bodied' either as coaches or as dual-purpose vehicles (semi-coach seats in a bus shell) whereas from 1962 the majority were built to the newly permitted length of 36 feet. Most of these longer Reliances carried coach bodywork although 39 received Marshall bus bodies before orders for single-deckers were switched to the rear-engined AEC Swift. Pictured on a Sunday morning at Dover, 610 escaped being painted into all-over white National coach livery, a fate which befell some of its less fortunate sisters. Thirty similar vehicles dating from 1962-63 were re-bodied, when eleven years old, with new Plaxton Panorama Elite coachwork as part of a plan to modernise the aging private hire fleet.

In 1971, to help alleviate a shortage of vehicles suitable for one-man operation, East Kent acquired thirty eight-year old Leyland Leopards which had become surplus to Southdown's requirements due to the arrival of new Daimler Fleetlines and Bristol VRs. When they arrived, the Marshall bodies contained only 45 seats due to a restrictive agreement that Southdown had with its trade union, so the second luggage pen over the nearside front wheel was removed to allow two additional pairs of seats to be fitted. In order to match moquette within vehicles, green seats were removed from four of the buses and distributed amongst the remainder. A further four sets of red seats were then salvaged from withdrawn AEC Reliances, one of which was a dual purpose vehicle with semi-coach seats. The lucky recipient of the more comfortable interior was 286 AUF, showing off its new coat of poppy red paint in the town of Folkestone, where all thirty Leopards were based.

Still looking smart at eighteen years old but soon to be withdrawn, 1957 AEC Reliance MU3RV MJG46 is kindly posed for the photographer by the obliging staff at Seabrook depot. The body, built by local coachbuilder Beadle of Rochester, has 41 seats and a central entrance, something that was becoming quite rare by this time. It was delivered as a 32-seater and originally had curved glass panels in the roof coving. Initially painted all-over dark red with a cream band, it acquired this red and grey scheme, unique to the Beadles, in 1972. Some of the batch even survived long enough to wear National Bus Company 'local coach' livery of poppy red with a white roof. As well as those for East Kent, Beadle supplied large numbers of coach bodies to Maidstone & District and Southdown, and the company also specialised in producing chassis-less vehicles to which were attached mechanical units of Commer and Morris-Commercial origin. In some cases, 'new' buses were constructed using parts salvaged from withdrawn pre-war Leylands and AECs.

Brown's Coaches of Ashford was concerned mainly with school and works contracts. The small, but smart, fleet included a pair of ex-Maidstone & District Harrington bodied AEC Reliances plus three second-hand double-deckers. The vehicle on the right, YJG807, is a 1962 AEC Bridgemaster 2B3RA which had not travelled very far from its original owner, the East Kent Road Car Company. The 72-seat front-entrance body was an integral part of the structure which supported the running units, mounted on detachable sub frames, in a similar fashion to the well known London Routemaster. AEC had hoped that this low-height, provincial version of the now iconic RM would prove a popular alternative to the Tilling Group's Bristol Lodekka but, by the end of its seven year production run, only 180 had been built. Alongside is a pair of Dennis Loline IIIs, numerically the first to be purchased by Aldershot & District in 1961, carrying Alexander 68-seat low-height bodywork. The Loline was of more conventional construction with a separate chassis actually based on the Lodekka design, the majority going to the Aldershot company. Note the 1964 Morris J2 van also painted in Brown's fleet livery.

Parked at the rear of Silverhill garage, on the outskirts of Hastings, and nearing the end of its eighteen-year life is 1958 AEC Reliance 2MU3RV 3359, demonstrating the effect of marrying a bus-type front to what was originally a Harrington 41-seat coach body. In 1955, Maidstone & District had embarked on a large OMO (one-man operation) conversion programme and during the mid-1960s, as a means of accelerating the demise of crew working, a batch of surplus coaches was adapted for bus work in this style. A powered two-leaf entrance door was fitted and a standard bus front grafted on in place of the more stylish original. The modifications resulted in the loss of one double seat. The vehicle was originally SC409 in the fleet numbering system in use between 1940 and 1968, where prefix letters denoted the type: D – double-deck, H – highbridge, L – lowbridge, S – single-deck and C – coach, with semi-coaches being classified SC. Standing alongside is one of the many highbridge Leyland Atlanteans with Metro-Cammell bodywork that Maidstone & District purchased between 1959 and 1963.

In February 1976 Maidstone & District began trials on routes in the Hastings area, comparing the performance of three different types of double-decker. Five 75-seat MCW/Scania BR111DH Metropolitans and five Ailsa AB57s were placed in service, alongside four of a batch of recently delivered Bristol VRs built to an increased height of 14 feet 6 inches. To add further variety, some of the VRs were powered by a Leyland 501 turbocharged unit in place of the more usual Gardner 6LXB engine. Inside Silverhill garage can be seen Ailsa 5383 and, just behind, Metropolitan 5254. The Ailsa was basically a Volvo product with a front-mounted turbocharged TD70 engine, in this case fitted with an Alexander 79-seat body. The ride could best be described as 'lively' as it lacked the refinement of air suspension, which was fitted to the Metropolitans it was operating alongside, and noise levels in the cab area were reminiscent of vehicles from a previous era. On the right is Leyland Panther 3120 with Strachans 49-seat front-entrance bodywork which, when new, possessed a separate exit door ahead of the rear axle. The elderly red vehicle is preserved 1937 East Kent Leyland Tiger TS8/Park Royal, JG 9938, in use as a mobile travel sales and enquiry office.

Although looking rather battered, 1951 Leyland PD2/12 NKT878 was still performing a useful role in Maidstone & District's small training fleet whilst at Silverhill depot in the summer of 1976. Delivered carrying fleet number DH382, the Leyland body originally had 58 seats and was fitted with electric platform doors to provide additional comfort for passengers travelling on longer routes, such as the 18 from Hawkhurst to Brighton or the 122 from Tunbridge Wells. Along with sister NKT875, it was converted for training use in 1970 when it became P2 in the number series reserved for ancillary vehicles. In the background can be seen the front of P3, previously 5477, a 1956 AEC Regent V also sporting training livery, and some of the essential components of the Gardner 6LX engine fitted at the rear of Northern Counties bodied Daimler Fleetline 6089. Resting on the bonnet of P2, is the driver's emergency escape window which, hopefully, was open merely to permit a little fresh air into the cab!

Basking in the sunshine outside Brook Street depot in Hastings is 1963 AEC Reliance 2MU2RA 3695 carrying a Harrington 42-seat front-entrance body. It is one of a batch of ten similar vehicles ordered specifically to provide extra capacity on the West Hill routes where narrow roads dictated the use of buses no more than 7 feet 6 inches wide. Also, to assist drivers in coping with the hilly terrain, the batch came equipped with semi-automatic gearboxes rather than the more usual synchromesh transmission. Maidstone & District favoured Reliances for bus work until 1966 after which deliveries switched to the rear-engined Leyland Panther. The Panthers were not a roaring success (excuse the pun) so vehicle policy changed again in 1970 to the Leyland Leopard, the 33 feet long PSU4 model becoming standard for the following three years. The background view gives an impression of the difficult operating territory in this well-known Sussex coastal resort.

Most bus companies run a number of support vehicles to assist with driver training, vehicle recovery or repair, parts collection, route monitoring and, in some cases, to provide refreshment facilities for the driving staff. Maidstone & District's fleet of around thirty ancillary vehicles included three recovery lorries, two of which were ex-War Department AEC Matadors, acquired around 1960. The third, P32, was an AEC Regal, YKT 959, pictured in the confines of Hastings garage. It is carrying a set of the company's trade plates and started life in 1937 as a 36-seater bus, registered DKT 20. The Harrington body has been quite severely cut down to permit the attachment of a crane whilst retaining part of the original saloon as crew accommodation and workshop. On the side panel, the traditional scroll fleet name is still proudly displayed, perhaps as a gesture of defiance to the National Bus Company's corporate identity manual.

Following batches of Leyland Titans and AEC Regent IIIs, some with rare Bruce coachwork, Eastbourne Corporation turned to the Regent V for its double-deck requirements. From the batch of five delivered in 1962 is no.65 (JJK 265) heading towards town at speed along the main thoroughfare known as 'Seaside'. It carries a 60-seat East Lancs body and was the first vehicle to be painted in the mainly cream livery adopted in 1969 as an alternative to the former deep blue and primrose. The centre of the roof is translucent, a feature introduced on Eastbourne's buses in 1961, which made travelling on the upper deck a very pleasant experience, especially in summer. Route 4 started from the 'Archery', a short walk from the Corporation's depot in Churchdale Road and therefore an ideal location for crew changes. A late model Triumph 2000 keeps a safe distance behind the bus whilst a BMC 1100 heads east.

Although the nearby Top of Beachy Head had long been served by Southdown Motor Services, Eastbourne operated a small number of open-top buses to the Foot of Beachy Head and along the seafront. For many years, a batch of five 1946 Leyland PD1s performed this duty, but they were withdrawn in 1968 and seafront services continued with closed-top buses, albeit with fully-opening windows on the upper deck. However, in 1973, six-year old Leyland Titan PD2A/30 no.84 had the roof removed from its 60-seat East Lancs body and holidaymakers could once again enjoy the delights of a ride along the front with the sun in their eyes and the wind in their hair. A new pale blue livery was applied and this still looked smart when the bus was passing the Pier on training duties in 1978, the 75th anniversary of motor buses in the town. No.84 was later joined by two ex-Ipswich Leyland Atlanteans converted to open-top but by 1989 it was surplus to requirements so was sent north to Blackpool Transport, who exchanged it for a closed-top Leyland PD3, LFR 532F.

In 1974 Eastbourne Corporation was retitled 'Eastbourne Borough Council' and eventually adopted a logo for its bus fleet known rather unkindly, in some circles, as 'Egg, Bacon and Chips'. Standing outside the depot in Churchdale Road is Leyland Panther no.1, one of thirteen delivered between 1968 and 1971, all with East Lancs bodies. Three outwardly similar buses on Daimler Roadliner chassis were also purchased but proved troublesome, like those in service with other operators. The Panthers performed adequately but the elderly residents of the town preferred to have a seat rather than stand, so future orders were for Atlantean double-deckers. Just around the corner from the depot could be found the strangely named Ecmod Road, the spelling of which was, in fact, derived from the initials of the Eastbourne Corporation Motor Omnibus Department. The fine red-brick building has now gone and the present-day fleet operates from a new depot in Birch Road. The company has recently been the subject of a takeover by Stagecoach.

After a four-year fling with high capacity saloons, Eastbourne turned once more to the double-decker with no.11 (KHC 811K) the first of 27 Leyland Atlanteans delivered new between 1972 and 1980 (a few more were subsequently purchased second-hand). Early examples were on PDR1A/1 chassis but when the improved AN68 model appeared, the days of the Panthers were numbered. No.11 is working the 1/4 group of routes, having just left Langney District Shopping Centre for the town centre and Old Town. It will return as a 14A to Winkney Farm and then run back into town showing service 1 before retracing its steps as a 4A to Marsden Farm. Some route numbers were used in one direction only, a fact that must have caused some confusion for visitors and, possibly, the driving staff. On the platform of the East Lancs 76-seat body stands a Corporation driver on his way to the depot to start an afternoon shift. Note the size of the 'Exact Fare Please' sign below the windscreen.

Attending the 22nd British Coach Rally on Madeira Drive, Brighton, in April 1976, is ex-East Kent AEC Regent V PFN 879, in use as a promotional vehicle for National Travel (South East) Ltd, the NBC's London-based coaching unit. The 72-seat Park Royal body was converted to open-top by East Kent for its route 69, serving Thanet coastal resorts, but when the vehicle became surplus to requirements in 1975 it passed to NT(SE) suitably repainted for its new role. As well as operating National Express services the company ran an extensive programme of British and Continental tours under the 'National Holidays' banner as well as the cheaper 'budget' tours marketed as Ensign Holidays, some of which are being promoted on the excursion boards leaning against the side of the bus. After the show, the author recalls driving this vehicle back to Southdown's Freshfield Road garage, where it was parked overnight prior to returning to Catford the following morning. Also evident in this view are three early examples of coachwork by Spanish builder Salvador Caetano, imported into the UK by Alf Moseley and marketed under the 'Moseley Continental' name.

Waiting at Brighton Station ready to depart on another round-trip on route 42 is 1963 Leyland PD2/37 no.25, one of 30 such examples operated by the Corporation. The 64-seat Weymann body is wearing the first version of the blue livery introduced in 1970 and carries the obligatory 'Vokins' advert in the window over the rear wheel. When one-man operation of double-deckers became legal in July 1966, Brighton was the first operator to seize the opportunity and over the following months converted all its front-entrance PD2s by moving the bulkhead window forward and fitting a ticket machine and change tray in the narrow gap created. The arrangement was not ideal, with drivers complaining of back and neck pains as they had to twist around in the cab to issue tickets. Nevertheless, the fleet was augmented in 1968 by five longer Leyland PD3/4 half-cabs already constructed with one-man operation in mind. Oddly enough route 49, which was operated with Atlanteans from 1971, had two-man crews until the last of the conductors were phased out.

After the PD2s and PD3s, Brighton had a brief flirtation with single-deck buses, purchasing seven Leyland Panther Cubs in 1968, four with Marshall bodies and the remainder with rather more attractive Strachans coachwork like no.36, waiting to take up service in Old Steine. They replaced the last of the Weymann AEC Regents delivered after the war, but were nowhere near as popular with the transport department and all were disposed of when their seven-year Certificates of Fitness expired. It would be another eight years before saloons appeared again, this time in the shape of Leyland National 2s for the Mile Oak Shuttle service. In this view, the solitary intending passenger braces himself against the elements whilst the driver tries to appear busy in the comparative warmth of his cab. It will be noted that Brighton was very keen on utilizing as much of the panelling as possible for the display of revenue-earning advertisements.

After the Panther Cubs, Brighton realized the advantages of operating rear-engined double-deckers, ordering several batches of Leyland's tried and trusted Atlantean model. The first two batches carried bodywork by Willowbrook, to a rather dated design, and were fitted with unusually narrow seats. Whilst these allowed a certain freedom of movement for the conductor, due to the wider gangway, it meant that some passengers endured a rather precarious ride balanced on one cheek! In 1975, ten AN68 Atlanteans arrived, this time with better-appointed East Lancs bodies like no.59, displaying the revised version of the blue and white livery, at the bottom of Elm Grove. The separate exit door was a feature intended to speed boarding and alighting, although this did not solve the age-old problem of passengers rummaging about for change rather than having the money ready in advance. One can only speculate as to the driver's thoughts as he patiently waits for the elderly lady to extract the requisite coins with which to purchase her ticket. More East Lancs Atlanteans were delivered in 1977 and 1978, the final batch with 74-seat single-door bodywork and fully-automatic gearboxes.

Pulling away from Churchill Square, on a two-week trial with Brighton Corporation, is Coras Iompair Eireann Leyland Atlantean AN68 D694 with Van Hool-McArdle 74-seat bodywork built at the former C.I.E. Spa Road works in Dublin, one of 219 purchased by the Irish state operator. The plain styling is certainly not enhanced by the livery, which rather reminds one of the new generation of 'colours' introduced in 1972 by British Leyland for its Mini, Allegro and Marina ranges of cars. The big windows did make for a light and airy interior however. It would seem that during the period of the loan, the Corporation had to supply its own tyres, as the bus sports blue split-rim wheels rather than the tubeless variety coming into fashion at the time. In the background is the famous Clock Tower which agrees with the clock above Debenhams entrance that it is ten minutes to two. Compare this fairly quiet scene with Churchill Square nowadays!

Belonging to the British Electric Traction group, it was inevitable that Southdown Motor Services Ltd. would possess a quantity of single-deck buses fitted with BET standard design bodywork. This was supplied by several manufacturers including Weymann of Addlestone as was the case with 'car' 151 photographed in Pool Valley, Brighton in 1974. The chassis is a Leyland Leopard PSU3/1RT, the 'T' denoting the fitting of an Eaton two-speed rear axle unit enabling the vehicle to feel equally at home on urban and rural routes. The observant reader will note the almost complete absence of window ventilators, save for one just visible on the offside, which was a result of the company specifying its unique underfloor heating and ventilation system (UHV). This theoretically offered passengers a perfectly controlled climate in which to enjoy their journey but, in practice, the buses proved to be hot in summer and cold in winter with later batches reverting to a more conventional arrangement. No.151 has received a more subtle cream version of the new NBC style fleet name although it still bears original Southdown livery including the moulded fibreglass nameplate under the windscreen. The accident-damaged front corner emphasizes the rural nature of the Lewes area routes.

Southdown House, the company's head office, was in Freshfield Road, Brighton. Running parallel is Queensway, and on a misty morning Bristol Lodekka FS6B 2069 (ENJ69C) is nearing the top after a long climb in second gear. The 60-seat Eastern Coach Works body clearly displays the air intakes for the Cave-Brown-Cave heating system which dispensed with the normal engine compartment radiator but produced a tendency to boil over, especially on steep hills such as this. The destination blind shows 'Race Hill' so the vehicle has only another 300 yards to travel before reaching the point where it will stop to cool down. The photographer is standing on a grassy mound at the edge of the site of Whitehawk Camp, an ancient hill fort, and behind him is Manor Hill, which crosses Brighton Racecourse. On race days, turf is laid across the road surface and buses on route 44 heading for Black Rock drive up over the turf when the marshals open the road between races. Note the relatively small number of parked cars in this less affluent part of the town.

Twenty Bristol Lodekka FLF6Gs were inherited following the absorption of Brighton, Hove & District, upon the formation of the National Bus Company in 1969. The first of these, numerically, is in London Road Brighton on service 5 to Patcham. Whilst the eight newest FLFs were exchanged with Bristol VRs from Eastern Scottish, 2073 continued in service on the south coast becoming one of only two of the type to receive Southdown green and cream livery. There is a hint of its original ownership in the red paint exposed following the loss of the 'Lodekka' badge from the bottom of the radiator grill. Eastern Coach Works built the 70-seat body, the general design of which was adapted for use on subsequent rear-engined Bristol double-deckers. Prior to its withdrawal in 1977, this bus could occasionally be seen plodding up and down between Brighton and Worthing, in company with Leyland PD3s, on the last crew-operated route from Worthing depot, the 230.

With the gradual disappearance of the Lodekkas, the ex-BH&D garages were allocated two batches of Northern Counties bodied Daimler Fleetlines, the first of which came in 1970 with Gardner 6LX engines and a distinct reluctance to climb hills. Although 33 feet in length, the ten vehicles only possessed 71 seats, thus offering Brighton's bus passengers generous leg-room. In 1972 a further fifteen were delivered, this time with the more lively Leyland O.680 unit and one of these, no.2120 (VUF 320K), is seen on a miserable wet evening waiting to depart Old Steine for the large Hollingbury estate to the north of the town. Following incidents of brake fade, one of which the author personally experienced, Daimlers were replaced on the 26/46 route in 1980 by Bristol VRs which had much superior stopping-power. One unusual aspect of some of Southdown's Brighton one-man routes around this time was the retention of conductors, who would board the bus during the morning peak and work to around five p.m. The driver would collect the fares during the early morning and again, after the conductor had cashed up and gone home for his tea.

Rural routes were generally in decline thirty years ago but one such operation introduced in 1976 was the Wednesdays-only 289 from Kirdford to Brighton via Billingshurst, Storrington and Steyning. The service consisted of one journey only, in each direction and a pair of Ford A0609s, carrying quite stylish Alexander 27-seat 'Midibus' bodies, was acquired for it. On Fridays, one of these buses would operate the 288, Kirdford to Chichester, also comprising a single journey each way. Performance was not lively, and due to the nature of the routes the Allison fully-automatic transmission was not used to its full potential. Running costs were disproportionate to the number of seats available and in spring 1977 the vehicles were sold to Western National. No.651 is in Pool Valley, Brighton, waiting to take villagers home after a morning shopping expedition. The Leyland PD3, alongside, is one of a number fitted with 'Rotavents' which were supposed to provide ventilation without draughts although, when closed, they tended to fill up with rainwater so that the first unwary passenger to seek fresh air received a wet shoulder as a result.

Climbing away from Hangleton on service 77, on its way to the popular tourist attraction of Devils Dyke, is one of Southdown's thirty convertible open-top Leyland PD3s, 406DCD, now numbered 3206 in a special series for fully depreciated vehicles (FDVs). These buses, delivered in 1964, replaced a fleet of wartime Guy Arabs de-roofed for use on summer seasonal services to Beachy Head and Hayling Island seafront. They outlasted their closed-top brethren by many years. Following delivery of a similar number of Bristol VRs which also had removable roofs, most were withdrawn by 1987, their registrations being transferred to other vehicles. Nevertheless, a healthy number survive today in the hands of preservationists including the subject of this picture, which was caught on camera in 1976. FDVs were buses retained in the fleet beyond their planned retirement date and were therefore of only nominal value in the company's accounts. Their mileage was restricted and maintenance was kept to a minimum, but this unfortunately meant that failure of a major unit such as an engine or gearbox inevitably spelt the end of the road and a one-way trip to the scrap yard!

Maidstone & District buses ventured as far west as Brighton on service 219, worked jointly with Southdown, and Leyland Atlantean AN68/Park Royal 5716 is about to make the long return journey back to Tunbridge Wells. The departure bays in Pool Valley were constructed in the days of rear-entrance buses (referred to as 'back loaders' by the staff) and passengers therefore had to walk between vehicles in order to pass the driver, who was of course, now collecting the fares. The absence of a conductor raised several safety concerns, and a banksman was therefore employed to assist drivers when reversing onto the stand. In a scene that would certainly be frowned upon today, the banksman, dressed in distinctly non high-visibility clothing, checks his departure sheet to see if the anxious looking passengers have much longer to wait before being allowed to board. The 'Wanderbus' map on the side of the bus includes the places covered in this book and it is of interest that in 1974 the enterprising traveller could 'wander' all day throughout such a large area for what now seems the modest sum of 60 pence. However, in real terms this was still what you would have expected to pay for two pints of decent beer.

In addition to the twenty-five long-wheelbase Fleetlines operating on Brighton area services, Southdown possessed two batches of fifteen single-door 30-foot examples with either Northern Counties or Eastern Coach Works bodies. In Bognor Regis bus station yard, examples from each batch are present, with the ECW version on the right. Allocated to Chichester, Bognor, Worthing and Horsham they also differed from their Brighton-based cousins in not being fitted with power steering, the absence of which made them very unpopular with drivers once the more refined series 3 Bristol VRs appeared on the scene. As a result, all thirty were sold, in 1980, to Crosville Motor Services Ltd., where they received a similar reception from the driving staff at Chester. Evident in this view is the push-up glass ventilation hatch on the rear roof dome of the NCME vehicles, screwed shut and painted over on 384, and the rather quaint 'target' device hanging from the canopy, which was supposed to assist drivers when reversing.

B. S. Williams Ltd., trading as Southern Motorways, was based in Emsworth and, as well as operating local services around that quaint fishing village, had a network of rural routes centred on Midhurst bus stand. Carrying the usual mid-day load associated with the Graffam service, WUR 867K, a 1972 Bedford YRQ with 45-seat Van Hool body awaits the return of its driver, who is probably taking a break in the High Street tea rooms. Southern Motorways ran eight of these vehicles, seven with wide doorways for bus work, and they effectively ousted the last of the fleet of ex-London Transport GS-class Guys for which Mr. Williams' company had become well known. However, the Bedfords were not without their problems and, following a series of brake failures, the whole batch was traded in for Fords after only three years use. The operator blamed the failures on the rather primitive vacuum-hydraulic system, derived from earlier designs, but the manufacturer attributed them to poor maintenance. The livery was inspired by a batch of vehicles, destined for Irish operator CIE, under construction at the Van Hool factory at around the same time.

Unattended one Sunday afternoon at their Emsworth base are three members of the fleet of seven Ford R1114 grant-coaches taken into stock by B. S. Williams Ltd. as replacements for the ill-fated Bedford YRQs. The yard was quite cramped and was situated down a residential cul-de-sac opposite Emsworth railway station. At the end of each day's work, vehicles had to be driven onto the fuelling bay, fuelled, then reversed out into the street to be turned around and finally reversed back into the yard again. A queue of returning buses often built up, much to the annoyance of local residents deprived of access to their favourite parking spots. As can be seen through the windscreens of the 53-seat Plaxton Panorama Elite bodies, the ticket machines were left in place over the weekend suggesting that fare collection on Southern Motorways was not an exact science. On the right of the picture, the sign just visible by the fuel pump reads 'Try Your Brakes', and is a reminder of difficulties experienced with previous makes of chassis.

Also based in Emsworth, as the name implies, is Emsworth & District Motor Services which celebrated its thirtieth anniversary in 2007. The first vehicle owned, 103 HPH, was a 1959 Bedford SB1 with a Bedford 300 series diesel engine and 41-seat Plaxton Consort body, acquired from Orange Coaches of Watford. It was not particularly fast and caused drivers considerable left shoulder ache due to the positioning of the gear lever behind the front-mounted engine. The Harrington seats, though obviously not original fittings, were actually very comfortable and initial concerns, apparent as hirers watched the vehicle draw up, were invariably dispelled by the end of the journey, often resulting in repeat business. The company eventually moved on to more modern rolling stock, branching out into stage-carriage and school contract work, and the fleet now stands at around twenty vehicles. In this 1978 view, the Bedford is on loan to Hellyers Coaches at their Fort Wallington, Fareham base.

This is not, as it might appear, a corner of a Barnsley breaker's yard, but actually the parking area at the side of Southdown's Hayling Island garage, once home to a staff of forty drivers and conductors but nowadays a hardware store. Reflecting on their fates, in autumn 1974, are withdrawn Northern Counties bodied semi-automatic Leyland PD3/5s 935, 943, 946 and 918 whilst another from the same batch looks on. A staunch Leyland customer, Southdown continued to buy this combination (although mostly with manual gearboxes) until 1967 by which time it had accumulated a fleet of 285. Other operators had already eschewed the traditional mechanical layout in favour of the rear-engined Atlantean and Fleetline. One-man operated buses eventually became the order of the day and the last conductor disappeared from the company's Western Division routes in 1976, with the remaining PD3s transferred to Brighton as replacements for rear-entrance Bristol Lodekkas. Of the four vehicles identifiable in this picture, 943 and 946 were exported to Hong Kong for further service with the China Motor Bus company and lived on, in one form or another, until the mid-1980s.

The year 1977 saw many operators turning out a selection of vehicles in commemorative liveries to celebrate Her Majesty The Queen's silver jubilee. Along with London Transport, the National Bus Company chose an all-over silver scheme with the cost of decoration being sponsored by large retailers, in this case Woolworths. As the silver finish was applied by spray gun, Southdown took the precaution of also preparing a selection of spare body panels in case the Atlantean or two Bristols so treated should suffer accident damage. The camera catches 'car' no.566 (GNJ 566N), a Bristol VRT/SL2 with 74-seat Eastern Coach Works body, pulling away from Hilsea Lido on stopping route 331 to Havant and Emsworth via Cosham (a direct journey to Havant was possible on limited-stop service 700). In the background is Southdown's Hilsea garage, dating from the 1930s, and the boarded up Bastion filling station, situated at the end of the Napoleonic ramparts which were, of course, constructed much earlier!

Being a Tilling Group company, Brighton, Hove & District was an enthusiastic user of the Bristol/ECW combination and, upon the amalgamation of the company with Southdown in 1970, some former BH&D vehicles found themselves sent forth to pastures new. In 1974, the first of the new Portsmouth area limited-stop services was introduced in the shape of the 740 route from the city to Wecock Farm housing estate. Initially, three Northern Counties bodied Leyland Leopards were allocated to the service but it soon became apparent that elderly passengers, or mothers with shopping and push-chairs, had difficulty climbing the steep entrance steps on these dual-purpose vehicles. After a few months, therefore, three Bristol RESLs were drafted in as replacements and, due to their low seating capacity and large standing area, soon became known locally as 'cattle trucks'. Following the further re-organization of Southdown's Portsmouth area services, the REs were transferred to lighter duties and 2209, about to pass the depot in Winston Churchill Avenue, has just arrived from HMS Dryad, Southwick, on a works special service. The destination blind has been wound to the end of the section containing the limited-stop routes, and is therefore displaying a blue blank. Limited-stop blinds had previously been red, but the colour was changed following a request from the local police, who had objected to buses showing a red light to the front.

Southdown was famous for its large coaching fleet, members of which could be seen all over Britain as well as on tours of the Continent and, from the earliest days, the company referred to its vehicles as 'cars'. 'Car' 1236, parked behind Winston Churchill Avenue (previously Hyde Park Road) depot, was one of those delivered primarily for excursions and express services, and therefore contains 49 seats rather than the 28 or 32 fitted in the more luxurious touring coaches. Plaxton built the Panorama body devoid of brightwork, at Southdown's request, and the Leyland Leopard chassis boasts air suspension and an Eaton two-speed rear axle for flexibility of performance. The grey front wheel gives us a clue that National Bus Company standard livery is starting to appear and the two vehicles in the background, a Weymann Castilian and a Harrington Cavalier, will soon become fond memories. 1236 went on to get NBC white coach livery, and other members of the batch were retained beyond their normal service life classified as FDVs (Fully Depreciated Vehicles) painted green and white for schools and works contracts.

With the instructor and his trainees taking a welcome lunch break, we find an ex-Brighton, Hove & District Bristol KSW6B, now numbered 2442, parked behind Winston Churchill Avenue coach station. The coaches are now in National white but presumably the 1952-built Eastern Coach Works body on the KSW was not deemed important enough for a repaint following its relegation to the status of training bus, and is therefore still in its former owner's livery. Even the red and blue NBC logo on the side advertisement seems despondent as it has been applied upside down, facing backwards! Southdown had three driving schools, at Portsmouth, Worthing and Conway Street, Brighton where this particular vehicle was based. Recruits destined for the ex-BH&D garages would need to master the intricacies of the constant-mesh gearbox, as there were still many Lodekkas in service so fitted. Similar vehicle 6447 (HAP 985) is now restored to pristine condition and operated by the present-day Brighton & Hove Bus and Coach Company on private hires and, occasionally, scheduled service work.

During the summer months visiting coaches often took advantage of the facilities at Southdown garages, and the driver of Crosville Bristol RELH6L no.CRL 262 waits for some of his passengers to return to the parking area at the rear of Winston Churchill Avenue. Why he decided to drop them off here, particularly, is anybody's guess as a dry pathway with proper kerb was available just around the corner. The little wooden footstool is a nice touch but is an item seldom used nowadays because of the inevitable health and safety implications. The 49-seat Eastern Coach Works body looks particularly smart and still sports the illuminated fleet name panel above the front wheel, a reminder of its previous days in cream and black. A green painted Harrington Cavalier, soon to be withdrawn, stands as reserve in the background, whilst a slightly newer Grenadier model is given fresh hope by the application of the new NBC white coach livery.

'Solenteer' was the name given to the joint Southdown/Hants & Dorset limited-stop route X71 between Southsea and Southampton. Standing in the sun at South Parade Pier is Series 3 Bristol VRT 3341, waiting to operate one of the alternate short workings to Fareham via the new M275 motorway. Few passengers are evident in this lunchtime scene, presumably preferring to catch the 347 behind, which will take nearly twice as long to reach Fareham but will serve many places along the way. Southdown's share of the X71 was handled, at this time, by new Park Royal bodied Leyland Atlanteans. The wooden hut on the right of the picture was occupied by the Control Inspector, who would oversee the timely departure of buses to destinations north, east and west of Portsmouth, as well as serving tea to thirsty bus crews. In winter, they would huddle inside from the cold until it became almost impossible to open the door. The hut has now gone, along with the recess it occupied in the promenade wall. The route has changed over the years, becoming the X16 and then 727, with a variety of operators including Portsmouth Citybus, Southampton Citybus, Tellings Golden Miller and Solent Blue Line.

Accelerating its abandonment of the trolleybus, City of Portsmouth Passenger Transport Department was in need of a large number of high-capacity vehicles on which former trolleybus drivers could quickly be retrained without the necessity of mastering a manual gearbox. The new Atlantean PDR1 was the obvious choice, as Portsmouth had been a loyal Leyland user for a number of years. Thirty-five arrived in 1963, numbered 201 to 235, followed by further batches up until 1966, by which time a total of 54 had been taken into stock. The 76-seat bodywork was by Metro-Cammell, and incorporated a gradually curving staircase and stepless entrance platform, both features designed to speed boarding and alighting (low floor buses are nothing new!). When delivered, a Leyland-designed centrifugal clutch was fitted to the semi-automatic gearbox, but this could not stand up to the punishment caused by ill-timed gear changes which were possible with this type of transmission, so this was quickly changed to the more durable fluid flywheel arrangement. In this view, 205 wears the brighter livery introduced in 1971, and is laying-over in Winston Churchill Avenue before returning to Cosham and Wymering as a 20, the opposite direction of route 19.

In 1967, following delivery of the 54 PDR1 Atlanteans, Portsmouth again turned to the dual entrance/exit single-decker as part of its OMO conversion programme, augmenting its ten Tiger Cubs and 19 Leopards with a batch of 26 Leyland Panther Cubs. They came fitted with either Marshall or MCW 42-seat bodies and one of the former can be seen behind AEC Swift 181, parked on The Hard facing the dockyard main gate. Panther Cub production ceased after 1968 so twelve Swifts were purchased, as the nearest equivalent 33-foot long chassis available (Portsmouth had tried 36-foot demonstrators but found they were too long to perform the required U-turn at the dockyard gate). One unusual feature of this city's two-door buses was a treadle-operated exit-door mechanism. Alighting passengers were faced with a notice which read 'To Open, Step Down', and once the driver had opened the front doors the weight of a passenger standing on the exit step would cause the rear doors to open too. Unfortunately, there was only a six-second delay before the doors slammed shut again, and some elderly Southsea residents were not nimble enough to extract their limbs before becoming trapped. The device was therefore removed in 1976.

The Leyland Atlantean in single-deck form was an unusual beast with, apart from Portsmouth, only Great Yarmouth and Birkenhead purchasing examples new. More recently, of course, some companies have had former double-deckers rebuilt to single-deck layout. With the demise of the Panther Cub model, and the high operating costs of the Swifts, the city's transport committee was left with little choice in what to buy from the Leyland stable so, in 1971/72, twelve Atlantean PDR2/1 chassis were delivered fitted with 40-seat single-deck bodies by Pennine, the coachbuilding division of Seddon. Whilst quite attractive when viewed from the front, the other end was rather ugly with featureless panels concealing the vertical 0.680 engine, above which were perched the occupants of the rear seat. The bodies were rather flimsy and due to the harsh ride (caused by springs intended to support the weight of two decks) their use was eventually confined to a ferryport service towing ex-British Airways luggage trailers. Latterly, three of the batch were transferred, with seats removed, to Portsmouth Ferryport ownership for use as dockside transfer vehicles. In this view no.195, in original livery, is laying-over at St Luke's church before returning to Portchester on route 145.

In 1972, after a five year love affair with single-deckers, Portsmouth returned to the Atlantean with the first of 100 of the improved AN68 type, carrying 75-seat Alexander bodies. Initially, a direct air-operated gear selector was fitted which, although producing a slight delay in gear engagement, resulted in smoother changes. With the last 35 buses, however, came fully-automatic transmission and the luxury of power steering! It is doubtful whether the separate exit door actually saved any time as it was placed so far forward, and after the first three passengers had paid their fares to the driver, their progress into the bus was invariably halted by the stream of people coming down from the upper deck. Three-year old no.261 (VTP 261L) is negotiating Hilsea roundabout on route 148, from Leigh Park estate to The Hard, a destination previously shown on Portsmouth buses as 'Dockyard'. Leigh Park is actually in the borough of Havant but responsibility for the provision of bus services fell to the Corporation after it acquired land on which to build 'overspill' housing. In the background is the new M27 flyover under construction, and a car that may not have survived long enough to use it!

Taking a break in a part of the city scheduled for redevelopment is no.126, the penultimate example of a long line of Portsmouth Leyland Titans dating back to 1930. It is a 30-foot long PD3/6 model, one of five delivered in 1959 carrying 70-seat rear-entrance Metro-Cammell bodies. In view of their length and generous interior leg-room the crews often referred to these buses as 'space ships' and by the time this one was photographed it had certainly reached its 'final frontier' having been relegated to training duties. Still evident is the smart lining out, a feature of Portsmouth buses from the earliest days, although now reduced to a simplified form. One unusual aspect of deliveries between 1952 and 1959 was the allocation of blocks of registration numbers ending in 999, with Titans in the GTP, LRV, ORV and STP batches so treated, plus the TTP Tiger Cubs which entered service in 1960. The instructor looks on as the new recruit takes his place in the cab for another stint behind the wheel.

In common with many operators, Portsmouth played host to visiting demonstration vehicles from manufacturers hopeful of securing orders for their latest products. The Ailsa underframe was constructed, employing Volvo mechanical units, at a new purpose-built factory at Irvine in Scotland, to a design favoured by long-serving fleet engineers. The engine was placed at the front, 'where it should be', and it was hoped that this layout would eliminate the failings normally associated with contemporary rear-engined double-deckers. This bus, part of a batch for South Yorkshire Passenger Transport Executive, carries bodywork by Van Hool-McArdle, a joint Belgian/Irish venture, well known for the many vehicles supplied to Coras Iompair Eireann during the 1970s and 1980s. A feature, much trumpeted in the trade press at the time, was the power output from the turbocharged Volvo TD70 engine. At 201 b.h.p., this made it the 'most powerful bus in Britain', ideal for climbing the hills around South Yorkshire. Pictured passing Southdown's Hilsea garage, it stayed in Portsmouth long enough to be fitted with local destination blinds but, in the event, the Corporation was not swayed and decided to continue with its policy of buying more of the tried and trusted Atlanteans.

As was traditional in many coastal towns, older double-deckers withdrawn from everyday service were often selected for conversion to open-top for the operation of summer seasonal services, usually along a suitable stretch of seafront promenade. By 1971, the four 1935 English Electric bodied Leyland Titan TD4s previously modified for this work were getting long in the tooth, and Portsmouth took the decision to gradually replace them with Metro-Cammell bodied PD2s rendered surplus by the arrival of new Atlanteans. Initially, four were converted, including no.104 (LRV996), which was renumbered 4 after losing its roof. A further two were similarly treated the following year when the TD4s were finally retired, all of them surviving into preservation. Five of the six PD2s were replaced in 1978 by cut-down twelve-year old Leyland Atlanteans, with only no.2 (LRV992) retained for special occasions. On a warm summer afternoon in 1977 no.4 has arrived at The Hard and the conductor changes the blind ready for the return journey. The commemorative livery, in celebration of Her Majesty the Queen's accession to the throne, has been achieved simply by adding a blue band and some transfers to what was the standard colour scheme for Portsmouth open-top buses. Having completed our whistle-stop tour of the major South Eastern bus operators, we can now join the crowds making their way up the ramp behind no.4 and board the ferry back to Gosport where, hopefully, our Provincial bus will be waiting.